Eggplant

The ultimate experience

Eggplant
The ultimate experience

R o s e m a r y   M o o n

NEW
BURLINGTON
BOOKS

Published by New Burlington Books

6 Blundell Street

London N7 9BH

Copyright © 1998 Quintet Publishing Limited

ISBN 1-86155-159-2

This book was designed and produced by

Quintet Publishing Limited

6 Blundell Street

London N7 9BH

creative director: RICHARD DEWING

art director: SILKE BRAUN

design: BALLEY DESIGN ASSOCIATES

designers: SIMON BALLEY AND JOANNA HILL

project editors: ALEXA STACE, DIANA STEEDMAN

photographer: IAIN BAGWELL

food stylist: LUCY MILLER

Typeset in Great Britain by

Central Southern Typesetters, Eastbourne

Manufactured in Singapore by United Graphic Pte Ltd

Printed in China by Leefung-Asco Printers Trading Ltd

contents

intro duct ion

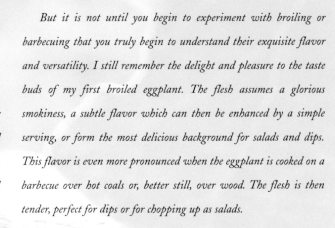

The eggplant is one the most popular of Mediterranean vegetables, and there is a growing number of eggplant addicts, eager to explore and experiment with one of the most versatile and delicious of vegetables. It is a common misconception that all eggplant dishes contain vast quantities of oil and must therefore be greasy, and doubtless also very bad for you. This simply is not true, and many dishes can be almost fat-free if the eggplants are broiled or barbecued in preference to being fried. All that is required to explore the versatility of the eggplant is a willingness to experiment.

Voluptuously rounded and smooth, the most common eggplants are the Mediterranean varieties which range from deep purple to pink in color, and often weigh upward of one pound. Roasted, baked or fried, they are the main ingredient in countless dishes, but can also be added as an extra, to turn an existing dish into something really special. Eggplants marinate well and readily absorb the flavors of seasonings and other ingredients, making them an excellent base for salads, dips and sauces.

But it is not until you begin to experiment with broiling or barbecuing that you truly begin to understand their exquisite flavor and versatility. I still remember the delight and pleasure to the taste buds of my first broiled eggplant. The flesh assumes a glorious smokiness, a subtle flavor which can then be enhanced by a simple serving, or form the most delicious background for salads and dips. This flavor is even more pronounced when the eggplant is cooked on a barbecue over hot coals or, better still, over wood. The flesh is then tender, perfect for dips or for chopping up as salads.

eggplants around the world

Many cuisines feature eggplants in their dishes, but Chinese, Greek, Indian, Italian, Thai, and Turkish cooking are especially associated with them. **Chinese** *dishes often include braised eggplants,* and they are especially useful for the numerous Buddhists who continue in a strict vegetarian tradition. Most recipes for Lo-han-style vegetables include, or may be augmented with, eggplants; the Lo-hans are minor

gods of the Buddhist faith, and this style of cooking originates in the many monasteries of China and Tibet.

In Japan *the eggplant forms a major part* of tempura, a dish of fish and vegetables dipped in a very light batter and fried in hot oil until crisp. In order to cook the eggplants as quickly as the other ingredients, long, thin varieties are favored over the plumper, Mediterranean ones.

Thai *cooking often features long, thin eggplants,* similar to those used for tempura, although there are popular green varieties which are a minimum of 20 inches long. Such shapes are ideal for slicing and cutting into large dice for salads. Another Thai variety which is very popular is the pea eggplant, which is very small and suitable for adding to dishes whole. These eggplants look very attractive, but are difficult to find in shops unless there is a large Eastern community in the area. The seed is also difficult to find, and I know many growers who are most anxious to find a reliable supply.

Rustic Italian *cooking is full of eggplants,* and many of the most famous dishes, such as caponata, are from Calabria in the south, known for robust and gutsy flavours. Long, thin eggplants are available in Italy as well as more rounded varieties; they are interchangeable in recipes as far as I am concerned, the shape being of more importance for presentation than flavor.

India *there are so many styles of* cooking in India that it is virtually impossible to make a blanket statement about the use of eggplants in Indian cuisine. They are, however, used extensively in main dishes and in a wide variety of pickles and preserves. The ability of the eggplant to absorb flavors from other ingredients makes it a valuable ingredient in curries, and the appearance of dishes is easily colored and enhanced by adding chile and turmeric, two important curry spices.

Greece *Moussaka is probably the best-known* of all European eggplant dishes. It originates in Greece, where it is usually made with minced lamb, topped with a white sauce or a goat's cheese cream. It is a sumptuous dish, and one which adapts well to being made with chicken, turkey or lentils. Other deservedly popular Greek dishes include dips of smoky eggplant, and marinated salads with garlic, olive oil, and parsley.

Provençal *food, with its robust Italian influence,* also makes full and bounteous use of eggplants. The mixture

of tomatoes, onions, zucchini, and olives is a natural medium for the eggplant, and any ratatouille or Niçoise-style dish is absolutely certain to be delicious.

Turkey *For many eggplant lovers* it is not until the delights of Turkish cooking are explored that the true glory of the vegetable is revealed. Some might argue that without the eggplant there is no Turkish cuisine; others might say that to eat in Turkey is to be sated with eggplants. Their dishes are full of the mystery of the smoky flesh, blended with tomatoes and oils and an inspired blend of spices. The Turkish style is, for me, an inspired mix of warm Mediterranean flavors and the spiciness of northern Africa and the Middle East.

history
Both India and China claim to be the original birthplace of the eggplant, although there are interestingly no records of it growing in the wild. However, it is likely that China was the source, and there are botanical references to the eggplant in records of Chinese market gardening dating from 500 BC.

It was certainly popular throughout Asia before it reached Europe in the Middle Ages. Like so many 'new' foods it was regarded with a good deal of scepticism and wariness, and was even referred to as the mad apple *or* apple of Sodom: *damning descriptions indeed. Until* little more than a hundred years ago, the eggplant was regarded by many botanists as a decorative plant, rather than one to eat and enjoy. What a lot they missed out on.

the many varieties of eggplant
Eggplants belong to the same family as potatoes, Solanaceae, as do tomatoes and peppers. This is the

deadly nightshade family, which might explain why eggplants have sometimes had a bad press. All members of this family contain certain amounts of toxins, and in eggplants they are at their height in the immature fruits, in the stems and leaves. It is interesting to note that fruits picked immature do not keep for longer than a few hours at peak condition; perhaps this is nature protecting us from our own greed and haste.

Many eggplants grow quickly to over one pound in weight. I refer to these as large eggplants, but smaller varieties have specific uses. Tiny finger eggplants, or the small white egg-shaped plants that gave rise to the popular name, are excellent for relishes and preserves, including jelly, which require whole fruits. Thai eggplants are best for Eastern-style cooking, especially if they are to be sliced and fried with other vegetables in dishes which require a uniform size for presentation. I would regard a medium-sized eggplant as one weighing about 12 ounces.

I cannot really comment on the flavor of differing varieties, because all those that I have used have been in peak condition and very freshly picked, but grown in the same medium. The flavors of fruits are usually governed by the soil in which they grow and the nutrients on which they are fed. A chef friend professes a preference for Italian-grown fruits, which he believes to be slightly sweet.

Although several varieties of eggplants may be available in markets where there is a diverse ethnic population, I have geared this book mainly to the supermarket shopper, and the recipes are therefore all possible with the purple varieties. Supermarkets are waking up to eggplant culture, and many are looking at round fruits for stuffing, striped ones for presentation and the longer purple varieties which work well for Eastern cooking. Because it is impossible for me to obtain tiny ones I have not included recipes for them. If you have ready access to such fruits, you will find appropriate recipes in Middle Eastern or Turkish cookbooks.

salting
I am constantly asked whether it is necessary to salt eggplants before cooking them, a technique used to extract any bitter juices from the flesh. In most cases it isn't, mainly because most commercial growers are now feeding the plants so that the fruits have no trace of bitterness. However, I do salt eggplants if I want to soften slices for molding around a mousse, for a shell that is to be stuffed and baked, or if I am intending to bake them whole. Salting is certainly not necessary before frying or broiling slices for most recipes.

buying and storing
It is essential to buy eggplants when they are really fresh, with a dark, shiny, and blemish-free skin. With most varieties, the darker the skin the better, as a reddish tinge can mean that the fruit has been left on the vine too long, allowing the seeds to start to develop which, in turn, will indicate that the flesh is more likely to be bitter.

In addition to sweetness of flavor, a fresh eggplant will have a much more tender skin. Someone once put it to me that eating a tough eggplant is like eating salami without first removing the skin: horrid! You should also check that the calyx is fresh-looking, and not shriveled or bruised.

As freshness is of such importance I would really recommend buying them as you need them. However, if you have to store them, they keep best loosely wrapped in a plastic bag in the salad drawer of the refrigerator.

growing eggplants at home

Eggplants make wonderful greenhouse plants, and I have grown them very successfully without heat. They do like a fair bit of humidity; I seem to succeed in providing this by splashing water around before the sun is too strong, a very untechnical application, I grant you, but it does work for me!

They seem to require high temperatures to set, especially the more unusual varieties. Once the fruits have set and the flowers have faded, make sure that the flowers fall free of the baby fruits. If they are left in contact and start to rot, the fruits will be blemished as well. Feed generously with a tomato fertilizer once a week once the fruits have set.

To encourage maximum growth it is a good idea to limit the number of fruits on each plant to between six and eight. Discard any baby fruits that you thin, remembering that immature specimens contain high levels of solanine.

complementary ingredients

As the eggplant is able to absorb the flavors of foods cooked with it, there are some ingredients which are natural partners and will always produce a successful dish when teamed together. These include:

Tomatoes *in all their forms: fresh from the vine, sun-dried, puréed or tomato paste. The acidity of tomatoes provides a marvelous base for eggplant dishes, and the color also greatly enhances the appearance of many eggplant dishes. Well-reduced tomato sauces also add a richness which requires enhancing with only a little olive oil.*

Olive Oils *to be used with eggplants may be rich, green, and fruity, or fragrant and light; the natural flavor of the aubergine will absorb and be enhanced by both.*

Rich Meats *By this I really mean meats with a useful amount of fat, which will not only flavor the dish but also keep the eggplants moist. For example, stuffed eggplants are always successful when filled with a ground meat filling, such as pork, lamb or beef, as the fat will soak down to the shells and encourage them to cook through in the oven. However, for chicken or vegetable fillings which are low in fat, I have found it necessary to add broth to the dish, to encourage the shells to bake tender. The natural richness of red meats also enhances the*

Mediterranean provenance of the eggplant.

Low-fat Foods *and eggplants go well together, but the eggplants generally require roasting, broiling or barbecuing before they are suitable for calorie-counted dishes. This will soften or completely cook the eggplants, allowing them to be diced or puréed for a wide variety of dishes, and completely dispelling any thoughts that they must always be cooked in large quantities of oil.*

If you intend to cook the eggplants very quickly you should prick them all over to prevent the skins from splitting. However, I find that they are better cooked a little more slowly and, by not pricking them, I have convinced myself that the smokiness is more pronounced. The eggplants are ready when the skin is blackened and blistered – it

will usually become quite crisp – and the flesh is soft. Eggplants need about 30 minutes to cook in a hot oven, at 400–425°F.

To make peeling easier, cover them with a damp cloth, which helps to steam the skins off. Leave the fruits covered for about 10 minutes, until cool enough to handle, then peel off the skins. Remember that it is always easier to peel fruits if you start at the flower end and not from the stalk; this also applies to tomatoes, peaches, and bell peppers.

appe

tizers

eggplant
humus

FOR ALL HUMUS FANS. THIS VERSION USES EGGPLANT IN PLACE OF CHICK PEAS, BUT THE TAHINI GIVES THE DIP THE FLAVOR THAT YOU WOULD EXPECT FROM HUMUS.

serves six

1 large eggplant

3 scallions, roughly chopped

1 red chile, seeded and chopped

Grated rind and juice of ½ lemon

2 garlic cloves, crushed

Salt and freshly ground black pepper

3 Tbsp olive oil, plus extra for drizzling

½ cup tahini

Paprika, to sprinkle

one Cook the eggplant on a barbecue, under a broiler or in a hot oven until the skin is wrinkled and blistered and the flesh is tender. Turn once or twice during cooking. Cover with a damp cloth and leave to cool for 10 to 15 minutes, then peel off the skin. **two** Chop the eggplant, then mix in a bowl with the remaining ingredients. Spoon into a small serving dish. Drizzle with a little extra olive oil and sprinkle with paprika. Serve with warmed pitta bread, or vegetable sticks for dipping.

eggplant
pesto

A RELATIVELY LOW-FAT PESTO WITH A HINT OF SMOKINESS FROM THE EGGPLANT.

serves four

1 large eggplant

1 large handful of fresh basil leaves

2–3 garlic cloves, roughly chopped

½ cup pine nuts

¾ cup freshly grated Parmesan cheese

1 tsp coarse sea salt

¼ cup olive oil

one Cook the eggplant over a barbecue, under the broiler or in a hot oven until the skin is wrinkled and blistered and the flesh is tender. Cover with a damp cloth and leave to cool slightly for about 10 minutes, then peel off the skin. **two** Blend all the remaining ingredients together in a blender or food processor, then add the eggplant and blend again. Season to taste. Serve tossed into freshly cooked pasta.

minted eggplant salad with yogurt

A CREAMY SALAD TO SERVE WITH COLD ROAST MEAT OR POACHED SALMON. I LIKE TO SPICE IT UP A BIT WITH TOASTED CUMIN SEEDS, BUT FENNEL OR CORIANDER SEEDS WORK JUST AS WELL.

serves **four to six**

1 Tbsp cumin seeds
½ cup fruity olive oil
1 large eggplant, sliced
1 garlic clove, crushed
2 Tbsp chopped fresh mint
1 cup plain yogurt
Salt and freshly ground black pepper

one Heat a large, ridged skillet over a moderate heat, then add the cumin seeds and dry roast for 30 seconds or so, until fragrant and just starting to pop. Transfer to a saucer and leave until required. **two** Heat the oil in the skillet, then add the eggplant slices and fry on both sides until lightly browned and tender. Do not be tempted to add more oil as some will run from the eggplant as it cooks. Remove the slices from the skillet and allow to cool a little, then place them in a shallow dish, sprinkle with the cumin, garlic, and mint and leave until cold.

three Spoon on the yogurt and season well. Serve lightly chilled.

eggplant guacamole

FOR ALL DIET-CONSCIOUS LOVERS OF MEXICAN FOOD! THIS IS A LOW-CALORIE VERSION OF THE TRADITIONAL AVOCADO DIP.

serves **four to six**

1 large eggplant
1 avocado, peeled and finely chopped
Grated rind and juice of 1 lime
2 tomatoes, seeded and finely chopped
1 green chile, seeded and very finely chopped
1 Tbsp very finely chopped onion
1–2 garlic cloves, crushed
Salt and freshly ground black pepper
Olive oil, to drizzle
Paprika, to sprinkle

one Preheat the oven to 425°F. Prick the eggplant all over, then place on a cookie sheet and roast for 30 to 40 minutes, until wrinkled and tender. Cover with a damp cloth and leave to cool completely. **two** Peel the eggplant, then chop into small pieces. Blend to a fairly smooth paste in a blender or food processor, then turn into a small bowl. Toss the avocado in the lime juice, then add to the eggplant with the remaining ingredients. Stir carefully until well combined. Season generously with salt and pepper, then drizzle with a little olive oil and sprinkle with paprika. **three** Serve with tortilla chips or warm toast.

eggplant and cheese pâté

A CREAMY PATE TO SERVE WITH TOAST OR CRACKERS.

USE WHOLE CREAM OR LOW-FAT CHEESE ACCORDING TO YOUR CONSCIENCE.

serves **six**

1 large or 2 small eggplants
1 cup cream cheese
1 garlic clove, crushed
1 green chile, seeded and chopped
1 Tbsp tomato paste
Salt and freshly ground black pepper
Paprika, to sprinkle

one Cook the eggplant over a barbecue, under a broiler or in a hot oven until the skin is wrinkled and blistered and the flesh is tender. Turn once or twice during cooking. Cover with a damp cloth and leave to cool for about 10 minutes, then peel off the skin. **two** Blend the eggplant with the remaining ingredients in a blender or food processor. Season well, then turn into a serving bowl. Sprinkle with paprika, then chill for 30 minutes before serving.

RIGHT: *eggplant guacamole*

eggplant, fennel and walnut salad

THE SALTED WALNUTS REALLY BRING THIS SALAD TO LIFE, AND COMPLEMENT THE EGGPLANT AND FENNEL WELL.

serves **six**

¾ cup olive oil

1 fennel bulb, finely sliced, feather leaves reserved for garnish

1 small red onion, sliced

¾ cup walnut pieces

Sea salt and freshly ground black pepper

1 large eggplant, cut into ½-inch pieces

1 Tbsp red wine vinegar

1 tomato, skinned, seeded and chopped

1 Tbsp torn fresh basil leaves

one Heat 3 tablespoons of olive oil in a skillet and add the fennel and onion. Cook until just soft but not browned, about 5 to 8 minutes. Remove with a slotted spoon and place in a salad bowl. **two** Add 2 tablespoons of oil to the skillet, then stir in the walnut pieces and fry them for about 2 minutes, until crisp and browned but not burnt. Remove the nuts from the skillet with a slotted spoon and drain on paper towels. Sprinkle with salt and toss the nuts until well coated and cool. **three** Add 4 tablespoons of oil to the skillet, then add the eggplant and fry over a moderate heat until tender and browned on all sides. Remove from the skillet and add to the fennel and onion. **four** Add the remaining oil to the skillet with the red wine vinegar and a little salt and pepper. Heat, stirring, until it is simmering, then pour over the vegetables in the bowl. Toss lightly then leave to cool. **five** When the salad is still slightly warm, add the salted walnuts, chopped tomato and basil. Leave until cold, then serve garnished with fennel leaves.

spring rolls

A VARIATION ON THE POPULAR CHINESE DISH.

THESE SPRING ROLLS ARE MADE WITH PHYLLO PASTRY AND FILLED WITH BRAISED

EGGPLANT MIXED WITH CRISPY STIR-FRY VEGETABLES.

serves **four**

3 Tbsp peanut oil, plus extra for brushing

1 eggplant, sliced

1 small onion, finely sliced

3 Tbsp oyster sauce

½ cup water

2 cups prepared stir-fry vegetables

Salt

**8 sheets phyllo pastry, measuring about
7 x 12 inches**

Soy sauce

one Heat the oil in a pan, add the eggplant and onion and cook gently until the oil has been absorbed. Mix the oyster sauce with the water, add to the pan and continue to cook slowly for about 10 minutes, until the eggplant is tender. Remove from the heat and leave until cool enough to handle. **two** Preheat the oven to 400°F and lightly oil a cookie sheet. Mix the eggplant and onion with the stir-fry vegetables, adding a little salt if necessary. Fold the phyllo sheets in half and brush with oil to keep them moist. Divide the vegetable mixture between them, making certain that every roll has some eggplant. Sprinkle each one with a few drops of soy sauce. **three** Fold the bottom and sides of the pastry in over the filling, then roll the pastry up into a sausage, brushing the edges with a little oil. Place on the prepared cookie sheet and brush lightly with oil again. **four** Bake the spring rolls in the preheated oven for 10 to 15 minutes, until the pastry is browned and crisp. Serve immediately with soy sauce.

eggplant sandwiches

THIS RECIPE USES SLICES OF EGGPLANT AS THE 'BREAD' IN BAKED HAM AND CHEESE SANDWICHES. THEY TASTE DELICIOUS.

serves four

1 large eggplant, cut lengthwise into eight ¼-inch slices

Salt

Olive oil, for brushing

2 slices ham, smoked turkey, or cooked chicken

2 slices Cheddar or other sharp cheese

1 large egg, beaten

1 Tbsp milk

1½ cups fresh white bread crumbs

Salad leaves, to garnish

one Lay the eggplant slices on a cookie sheet in a single layer, then sprinkle salt over them and leave for 30 minutes. Rinse thoroughly under cold water and pat dry on paper towels. **two** Preheat the oven to 400°F. Brush the slices lightly with olive oil on the outsides, then assemble them into four sandwiches. Fill each one with half a slice of cheese and half a slice of ham, trimming them to fit so that the filling doesn't overflow. **three** Dip the sandwiches into the beaten egg, then into the breadcrumbs. Press on sufficient bread crumbs to give a good coating. Place the sandwiches on an oiled cookie sheet and bake in the preheated oven for 20 minutes, or until lightly browned. Serve immediately with a salad garnish.

eggplant cream

SOMETIMES CALLED *HÜNKÂR BEGENDI* OR SULTAN'S DELIGHT, THIS DELICATE CREAMY DISH IS SERVED AS A SAUCE FOR MEAT OR FISH, OR A DIP.

serves six to eight

2 large eggplants

1 Tbsp lemon juice

4 Tbsp butter

⅓ cup all-purpose flour

2 cups milk

Salt and freshly ground black pepper

¾ cup freshly grated Parmesan

Chopped fresh parsley, to garnish

one Cook the eggplants on the barbecue, under the broiler or in a hot oven until the skins are wrinkled and blistered and the flesh is tender, turning once or twice. Cover with a damp cloth and leave to stand for 10 to 15 minutes, then peel off the skin. Leave the eggplant flesh in a bowl of cold water with the lemon juice until required, to prevent discoloration. **two** Melt the butter in a large pan, then remove from the heat and stir in the flour. Cook slowly over a low heat for about 2 minutes, then put the pan to one side. Drain the eggplant and squeeze

dry with your hands. Add to the pan and blend either with a potato masher or with a hand-held blender. Gradually stir in the milk. **three** Bring the sauce slowly to the boil over a low heat, then season to taste. Simmer the sauce for about 15 minutes, or until it no longer tastes floury. Stir in the cheese, then season again if necessary. **four** Pour into a warm bowl or dish and sprinkle with chopped parsley.

thai salad

BRIGHT WITH THE FLAVORS OF THE PACIFIC, THIS IS AN EXCITING MAIN COURSE SALAD. USE HAM IN PLACE OF PORK IF YOU PREFER, AND MINT INSTEAD OF CILANTRO FOR A CHANGE.

serves **four**

2 long thin Thai or Japanese-style eggplants

2 hot red Thai chiles, seeded if preferred, and finely sliced

2 shallots, finely sliced

2 Tbsp fish sauce

Juice of two limes

1 Tbsp superfine sugar

½ cup finely chopped cooked pork

1 cup peeled shrimp, defrosted if frozen

2 Tbsp fresh cilantro leaves

one Cook the eggplants over a barbecue, under a broiler or in a hot oven until the skin is wrinkled and blistered and the flesh is tender. Turn once or twice while cooking. Cover with a damp cloth and leave for 10 to 15 minutes to cool. Meanwhile, mix together the chiles, shallots, fish sauce, lime juice, and sugar in a bowl. **two** Peel the eggplants and cut them into chunks. Toss the eggplants in the sauce, then add the pork and shrimp. Serve garnished with the cilantro leaves.

ratatouille

THIS IS MORE OF A SALAD, WITH THE VEGETABLES COOKED INDIVIDUALLY, BUT HAS ALL THE FLAVORS OF THE CLASSIC MEDITERRANEAN DISH.

serves eight as appetizer or four as a main meal

About 6 Tbsp olive oil
1 large onion, chopped
2 garlic cloves, finely sliced
1 green bell pepper, cored, seeded and sliced
1 zucchini, yellow if possible, sliced
1 long thin eggplant, about 2 inches in diameter, cut into ¼-inch slices
2 cups canned chopped tomatoes
⅔ cup red wine
4–5 sprigs fresh thyme
Salt and freshly ground black pepper
1 Tbsp freshly torn basil leaves
½ cup small black pitted olives
1⅓ cups diced feta cheese

one Heat 3 tablespoons of olive oil in a large skillet, add the onion and cook until softened but not brown, about 5 minutes over a medium heat. Add the garlic and cook for a few seconds longer, then remove the onion and garlic with a slotted spoon and place in a large bowl. **two** Add the bell pepper to the skillet and cook slowly for 4 to 5 minutes, then remove with a slotted spoon and place in the bowl. Add 1 to 2 tablespoons of oil to the skillet, then add the zucchini and cook for 3 to 4 minutes, turning once. **three** Remove the zucchini with a slotted spoon and add to the bowl. Add 1 tablespoon of oil to the skillet, then add the eggplant slices and fry gently until lightly browned on both sides. Remove the eggplant with a slotted spoon and add to the bowl. **four** Add the tomatoes to the skillet with the red wine and thyme, salt and pepper. Bring to the boil, then simmer gently for 5 minutes. Remove the thyme, then pour the hot sauce over the vegetables in the bowl. Leave to cool, tossing the vegetables in the sauce once or twice. **five** Just before serving, add the torn basil leaves, olives, and cheese. Serve at room temperature for the best flavor.

griddled eggplants with tomatoes and mozzarella

A SIMPLE BROILED DISH TO SERVE AS A MAIN COURSE SALAD OR AN APPETIZER, WITH CRUSTY BREAD TO MOP UP THE JUICES.

serves four

2 large eggplants, cut lengthwise into ¼-inch slices

Salt and freshly ground black pepper

⅓ cup olive oil

Small handful of fresh basil leaves, roughly torn

8 small ripe tomatoes, halved

2 garlic cloves, finely sliced

4½ oz mozzarella, drained and thinly sliced

1 tsp balsamic vinegar

one Make a single layer or the eggplant slices and sprinkle generously with salt. Leave for at least 30 minutes, then rinse thoroughly under cold water and pat dry with paper towels. **two** Pour the oil into a shallow dish. Dip each slice of eggplant into the oil, then cook the slices, a few at a time, in a griddle pan for 3 to 4 minutes on each side. **three** Layer the eggplant in an ovenproof dish with the basil, the tomatoes and garlic. Finish with a layer of eggplant, season well, then cover with the sliced mozzarella. **four** Add the balsamic vinegar to the oil left in the griddle pan and pour it over the cheese. Broil under a moderate heat for 4 to 5 minutes, until the cheese is bubbling and starting to brown. Serve with mixed salad leaves and bread to mop up the juices.

country grilled eggplant

AN ITALIAN-STYLE SALAD OF COOKED EGGPLANT SLICES MARINATED IN OIL AND MINT AND FINISHED WITH TOASTED PINE NUTS AND PARMESAN.

serves four

1 large eggplant, sliced thickly

Olive oil, for brushing

⅓ cup pine nuts, taosted

2 Tbsp chopped fresh parsley

Grated zest of 1 lemon

Shaved Parmesan cheese

one Preheat the broiler or griddle pan until very hot, then add the eggplant slices. Brush generously with olive oil, then broil or griddle until browned on both sides. **two** Mix together the ingredients for the marinade in a shallow dish. Add the eggplant slices and turn them in the mixture. Leave for 1 to 2 hours, then stir in the pine nuts. Serve at room temperature, sprinkled with the parsley, lemon zest, and Parmesan, with fresh crusty bread.

Marinade:

½ **cup olive oil**

1 garlic clove, crushed

12 large basil leaves, roughly torn

1 Tbsp chopped fresh mint

Salt and freshly ground black pepper

1 Tbsp balsamic vinegar

eggplant à la grecque

A MARINATED EGGPLANT SALAD WITH MUSHROOMS AND CHOPPED PARSLEY. SERVE WITH LOTS OF BREAD TO MOP UP THE DELICIOUS JUICES.

serves **four to six**

1 large eggplant, sliced

About ½ cup olive oil

Salt and freshly ground black pepper

1–2 garlic cloves, crushed

½ lb mushrooms, sliced

2–3 Tbsp chopped fresh parsley

one Preheat the broiler. Arrange the eggplant slices in the pan and brush with olive oil. Broil until browned, turning occasionally. **two** Place the eggplant slices in a serving dish and add enough oil to moisten, but not so much that they are swimming in it. Season well, add the garlic, mushrooms, and parsley and stir gently. Leave for 1 to 2 hours, then serve at room temperature.

eggplant with ginger

AN ASIAN SALAD TO SERVE WITH ANY CHINESE, JAPANESE OR THAI DISH.

serves **four**

2 large eggplants

2-inch piece fresh gingerroot

2 Tbsp light soy sauce

2 Tbsp sesame oil

1 Tbsp torn fresh cilantro leaves

Salt

Sugar, to taste

one Cook the eggplants on a barbecue, under a broiler or in a hot oven until the skin is wrinkled and blistered and the flesh is tender. Turn once or twice during cooking. Cover with a damp cloth and leave to cool for 10 to 15 minutes, then peel off the skin. Cut the flesh into large pieces and place in a bowl. **two** Grate the ginger coarsely, including the skin, then gather up the shreds in your hand, and squeeze the juice over the warm eggplant. Add all the remaining ingredients, stir well and leave for 10 to 15 minutes to marinate. Serve on a bed of lightly stir-fried carrot sticks, sugar peas, and bamboo shoots.

RIGHT: *eggplant with ginger*

eggplant
salad THIS IS BASED ON A TRADITIONAL NORTH AFRICAN RECIPE. PAPRIKA, ESPECIALLY
SWEET SPANISH PAPRIKA, IDEALLY COMPLEMENTS THE SWEETNESS OF THE EGGPLANT.

serves **four to six**

About 1 cup olive oil

2 eggplants, sliced

2 tsp sweet paprika

2 tsp ground cumin

2 garlic cloves, finely sliced

Grated rind and juice of 1 lemon

½ cup pistachio kernels

Salt and freshly ground black pepper

Sugar, to taste

one Heat ½ cup of oil in a large skillet and add the eggplant, paprika and cumin. Cook over a gentle heat so that the spices do not burn, adding more oil as necessary; the eggplant will take about 10 minutes to cook through. Add the garlic to the skillet halfway through the cooking. **two** Transfer the eggplant to a serving bowl, then add the pistachios, lemon rind and juice. Season well, adding a little sugar if you wish. Allow the salad to cool, then chill before serving.

eggplant
caviar EGGPLANT PASTES HAVE LONG BEEN REFERRED TO AS CAVIAR. NOTHING
LIKE THE REAL THING, BUT THE TEXTURE IS SIMILAR - A ROUGH PUREE WITH A TANG.

serves **four**

2 eggplants

Salt and freshly ground pepper

A little walnut oil

2 large tomatoes, chopped

1 large garlic clove, chopped

6 scallions

1 Tbsp freshly chopped oregano

2 hard-cooked eggs, finely chopped

one Preheat the oven to 425°F. Prick the eggplants all over, and place them on a cookie sheet and season lightly. Drizzle with a little oil, then bake for 30 to 40 minutes, or until tender. Leave to cool, then roughly chop the eggplants, including the skin. two Puree the eggplants in a blender with the tomatoes garlic, and scallions and enough oil to make a paste. Season well, then stir in the oregano and chopped eggs. Chill slightly, then serve with fresh hot toast.

caponata

THE REGION OF CALABRIA IN SOUTHERN ITALY IS FAMED FOR THE PUNGENCY OF ITS DISHES: EXCITING FLAVORS OF SIMPLE INGREDIENTS SKILFULLY BLENDED TOGETHER. CAPONATA IS ONE OF THE MOST FAMOUS OF ALL EGGPLANT DISHES AND THERE ARE MANY SUPPOSEDLY AUTHENTIC RECIPES FOR IT. THIS IS MY PERSONAL FAVORITE.

serves **four**

2 large eggplants, cut into ½-inch chunks

Salt

½ cup fruity olive oil

1½ cups mixed pickled vegetables, such as onions, gherkins, bell peppers etc, roughly chopped

⅓ cup capers

2 celery stalks, finely chopped

½ cup pitted green olives

1 Tbsp granulated sugar

⅔ cup red wine vinegar

2 Tbsp pine nuts

one Layer the eggplants in a colander with salt, then leave to stand for 30 minutes. Rinse thoroughly in cold water, then drain and pat dry on paper towels. **two** Pour all but 2 tablespoons of the oil into a large skillet, add the eggplant and cook for 10 to 12 minutes, or until browned and soft. **three** Pour the remaining oil into a small pan, add the pickles, capers, celery, and olives and cook slowly over a very low heat for about 10 minutes, until well softened. Add the sugar and vinegar and continue to cook slowly until the smell of the vinegar has gone. **four** Drain the eggplants of any excess oil, then add to the other vegetables with the pine nuts. Add a little salt to season, if necessary. Serve the caponata warm or cold.

eggplant
salad with cranberries
I HAVE USED CRANBERRIES IN THIS

RECIPE, BUT YOU COULD JUST AS WELL USE POMEGRANATE JUICE AND DRIED SEEDS INSTEAD.

THE SWEET TARTNESS OF THE FRUIT COMPLEMENTS THE EGGPLANT VERY WELL.

four to six

serves

3 Tbsp mild, fragrant olive oil

1 eggplant, cut into ¼-inch dice

1 small onion, finely sliced

½ cup cranberry juice

1 garlic clove, crushed

⅓ cup dried cranberries

Salt and freshly ground black pepper

⅔ cup toasted whole wheat bread crumbs

Chopped fresh parsley, to garnish

one Heat the oil in a skillet, add the eggplant and onion and cook over a moderate heat until the oil has all been absorbed. Add the cranberry juice and continue cooking until the eggplant is soft. Transfer to a serving bowl, add the garlic and allow to cool. **two** Add the dried cranberries and season to taste. Stir in the toasted bread crumbs and sprinkle with parsley just before serving.

eggplant
toasts
THIS IS A VARIATION ON THE EVER-POPULAR CHINESE SHRIMP TOASTS. THE

EGGPLANT CAN BE SHREDDED WITH A COARSE GRATER,

BUT YOU WILL FIND IT EASIER TO DO IT IN A FOOD PROCESSOR.

four

serves

4 slices white bread, crusts removed

Vegetable oil, for deep-frying

Finely chopped cucumber, to garnish

Thinly sliced chiles, to garnish

one Mix the eggplant with the remaining paste ingredients. Cut the bread into bite-sized triangles, then spread on one side with the paste. **two** Heat the oil to 320°F in a wok, then carefully add the triangles in batches with a spoon, paste side down, and fry for about 2 to 3 minutes, until the bread is golden brown. Remove with a slotted spoon and drain on paper towels. Keep warm until all the toasts are cooked. **three** Serve warm, garnished with sliced chiles and finely chopped cucumber.

ABOVE: *eggplant toasts*

Eggplant paste:

½ lb eggplant, peeled and shredded

1 egg white, lightly whisked

2 tsp sherry

2 tsp oyster sauce

Pinch of ground ginger

2 tsp cornstarch

Pinch of salt

fish
dis

hes

tuna and
eggplant kabobs

PERFECT FISH KABOBS FOR THE GARDEN OR BEACH BARBECUE OR TO BROIL INDOORS WHEN THE SEASON CHANGES.

serves **four**

1 lb 5 oz fresh tuna steaks, about 1 inch thick, cut into 1-inch cubes
1 long, thin, Japanese-style eggplant

Marinade:

Grated rind and juice of 1 lime
4 Tbsp olive oil
1 garlic clove, crushed
2 Tbsp chopped fresh oregano and parsley mixed
Salt and freshly ground black pepper

one Place the tuna in a glass bowl, then add all the marinade ingredients. Stir well and leave for at least 1 hour, stirring once or twice. **two** Half cook the eggplant on the barbecue or under the broiler, until the skin is just starting to wrinkle. Cut into ½-inch thick slices. Thread the tuna and eggplant on skewers, then brush with the remaining marinade. **three** Cook over a moderate heat for 5 to 6 minutes on each side, either on the barbecue or under a broiler, basting with any remaining marinade. Serve with a rice salad.

eggplant fish pie

THIS IS CALLED A FISH PIE, ALTHOUGH THERE IS NO PASTRY OR POTATO TOPPING IN SIGHT! INSTEAD, I HAVE MADE A TOPPING OUT OF SLICES OF GRIDDLED EGGPLANT OVER A FILLING OF MIXED SHELLFISH AND FILLETS OF FLOUNDER. IT MAKES A WONDERFUL SUMMER DISH.

serves **four**

2 large eggplants, cut lengthwise into ¼-inch slices

Salt and white pepper

3 Tbsp butter, plus extra for greasing

3 Tbsp all-purpose flour

2 cups milk

½ cup dry white wine

2 Tbsp snipped chives

2 cups mixed shelled shrimp and mussels, defrosted if frozen

½ lb fillet of sole, skinned and cut into 1-inch pieces

2–3 Tbsp olive oil

Paprika, for sprinkling

one Arrange the eggplants in a single layer on a cookie sheet, then sprinkle them with salt and leave for 30 minutes. Rinse thoroughly in cold water, then pat dry on paper towels. **two** Preheat the oven to 400°F. Melt the butter in a large pan over a moderate heat, then remove from the heat and stir in the flour. Cook gently for 1 minute, then gradually stir in the milk off the heat. Add the wine, then bring the sauce gradually to a boil. Season lightly and add the chives, then stir in the shellfish and flounder. Pour into a buttered ovenproof dish. **three** Heat a griddle pan or skillet and add the olive oil. Cook the eggplant slices in batches until browned on both sides, adding more oil if necessary, then arrange them on the fish in overlapping slices. **four** Bake the pie in the preheated oven for 20 minutes. Sprinkle with a little paprika before serving with creamy mashed potatoes and green vegetables.

salmon and eggplant kedgeree

I LOVE KEDGEREE, AND ESPECIALLY THIS ONE. I HAVE INCLUDED EGGPLANT AND SULTANAS, AND USED FRESH SALMON TO PROVIDE A GOOD COLOR CONTRAST TO THE EXTRA VEGETABLES. ADD A SPLASH OF CREAM IF YOU WISH, AND SERVE WITH A SPOONFUL OF MANGO RELISH FOR EXTRA SPICE.

serves **four**

1½ cups easy-cook long-grain rice

½ lb salmon fillet, skinned

4 Tbsp butter

1 Tbsp curry paste

1 onion, sliced

1 eggplant, sliced

3 hard-cooked eggs, chopped

⅓ cup raisins

Salt and freshly ground black pepper

Freshly chopped parsley, to garnish

Lemon wedges, to serve

one Cook the rice in plenty of boiling, salted water for 10 to 12 minutes, until tender. Drain thoroughly in a colander. **two** Poach the salmon fillet in a pan of barely simmering water for 4 to 5 minutes, until just cooked. Drain the salmon, allow to cool slightly, then flake, removing any bones. **three** Melt the butter in a large skillet with the curry paste. Add the onion and eggplant and cook for about 5 minutes over low heat, until soft. Add a little extra butter if necessary to keep the vegetables moist. Keep the heat low so that the spices do not burn. Add the rice and salmon to the pan, mix carefully and continue to cook gently for 2 minutes. **four** Add the chopped eggs to the kedgeree with the raisins, then season to taste. Serve garnished with chopped parsley and wedges of lemon.

trout with eggplant and cranberry sauce

EGGPLANT AND CRANBERRIES ARE A WINNING COMBINATION; THE CRANBERRIES BALANCE ANY OILINESS FROM THE EGGPLANT OR THE FISH.

serves **four**

4 Tbsp butter

2 Tbsp olive oil

1 eggplant, cut into ¼-inch dice

4 rainbow or brown trout, weighing 9–10 oz each

⅓ cup dried cranberries

3 kaffir lime leaves, finely shredded

2 Tbsp sour cream

Salt and freshly ground black pepper

one Heat 3 tablespoons of butter and 1 tablespoon of oil together in a large skillet, then add the eggplant. Cook for 3 to 4 minutes until lightly browned, then remove with a slotted spoon and keep warm in an ovenproof dish. **two** Add the remaining butter and oil to the skillet, then add the trout and fry them gently for 5 to 6 minutes on each side. Transfer them to a plate and keep warm in the oven while finishing the sauce. **three** Return the eggplant to the skillet and add the cranberries with the shredded lime leaves. Cook for 1 to 2 minutes, then add the sour cream. Continue heating until the cream has melted, season to taste, then serve with the sauce spooned over the fish.

lime-marinated swordfish with eggplant ribbons

SWORDFISH READILY ABSORBS THE FLAVORS OF MARINADES, AND I LIKE TO USE LIME FOR A REALLY FRESH TANG. RIBBONS OF FRIED EGGPLANT PROVIDE A STRIKING CONTRAST TO THE FISH.

serves **four**

4 swordfish steaks, about ½ inch thick and each weighing about 5 oz

3 Tbsp olive oil

1 small long eggplant, halved and sliced into fine ribbons

Marinade:

Grated rind and juice of 2 limes

3 Tbsp fruity olive oil

3 scallions, finely chopped

Salt and freshly ground black pepper

1 garlic clove, crushed

1 Tbsp chopped fresh parsley

one Mix all the ingredients for the marinade in a shallow dish, then add the swordfish. Leave to marinate for 1 to 4 hours, turning the steaks in the mixture once or twice. **two** Heat the oil in a large skillet. Drain the swordfish, reserving the marinade, then fry it quickly in the hot oil, allowing 2 to 3 minutes on each side. Remove the fish from the skillet and keep it warm. **three** Add the marinade to the skillet and heat it gently, then add the eggplant ribbons and cook quickly until they are soft and beginning to brown. Arrange the ribbons on the swordfish steaks before serving, spooning any remaining juices over the fish.

stuffed mussels

I FIRST DISCOVERED THE DELIGHTS OF STUFFED MUSSELS IN BRUSSELS, WHERE THEY HAVE RESTAURANTS THAT SPECIALIZE IN THEM. THE BEST MUSSELS FOR STUFFING ARE THE LARGE, GREEN-LIPPED VARIETY. THE ONES I BUY ARE FROM NEW ZEALAND AND VERY MEATY.

serves **four**

20 large green-lipped mussels, on the half shell

4 Tbsp olive oil

1 large onion, finely chopped

1 red chile, seeded and very finely chopped

1 small eggplant, very finely chopped

2 garlic cloves, crushed

Salt and freshly ground black pepper

¾ cup fresh whole wheat bread crumbs

Flat-leaf parsley sprigs, to garnish

one Preheat the oven to 425°F. Loosen the mussels on the half shells and arrange them on a cookie sheet. **two** Heat the oil in a large skillet. Add the onion and chile and cook until starting to soften, then add the eggplant and garlic. Continue cooking for 5 to 6 minutes, until all the vegetables are soft and lightly browned. Season well, then add the bread crumbs and mix thoroughly. **three** Pile a teaspoonful of filling into each shell over the mussel, then bake in the hot oven for 12 to 15 minutes, until piping hot. Serve immediately, garnished with flat-leaf parsley.

roast monkfish with eggplant and white wine sauce

THIS SOUNDS SOPHISTICATED, BUT IS VERY QUICK TO COOK. USE SOUR CREAM IF YOU PREFER IN THE SAUCE, BUT I FIND THAT ORDINARY CREAM REDUCES MORE SUCCESSFULLY.

serves three

1 monkfish tail, weighing about 1 lb 5 oz, filleted

2 Tbsp olive oil

Knob of butter, plus extra for greasing

2 tsp whole grain mustard

4 scallions, sliced

1 small eggplant, finely sliced

½ cup dry white wine

⅔ cup heavy cream

2–3 Tbsp fish stock or water

3 Tbsp snipped chives

Salt and freshly ground black pepper

one Preheat the oven to 425°F. Pull the papery skin away from the monkfish. Heat the oil and butter in a large skillet, then quickly fry the fillets on all sides. Place them on a buttered cookie sheet, then spread them with the mustard. Roast in the preheated oven for 12 to 15 minutes. **two** Add the scallions and eggplant to the skillet and cook quickly until the eggplant has absorbed the liquid. Add the wine and continue to cook until the eggplant slices are tender. Add the stock and cream and simmer until the sauce has reduced and thickened. Add the chives and season to taste. **three** Slice the monkfish fillets into thick medallions and arrange them on warmed serving plates. Spoon the sauce over the fish, and serve with sautéed potatoes and steamed green beans.

eggplant with gingered crab and vanilla pasta

A MOST UNUSUAL AND UTTERLY DELICIOUS DISH INSPIRED BY MY FRIEND PHILIP BRITTEN, THE MICHELIN-STAR CHEF AT THE CAPITAL HOTEL IN LONDON'S KNIGHTSBRIDGE. USE LOBSTER IN PLACE OF THE CRAB IF YOU WISH.

serves **four**

2-inch piece fresh gingerroot
1½ cups coarsely shredded crab meat
2 cups strong white bread flour
2 large eggs
A few drops natural vanilla extract
1 vanilla bean, split and seeds removed
⅓ cup light olive oil
1 eggplant, finely sliced
1-inch piece fresh gingerroot, peeled and finely chopped
1 tomato, skinned, seeded and chopped
Salt and white pepper

one Grate the larger piece of ginger, including the skin, with a coarse grater. Place the crab meat in a bowl. Gather up the shreds of ginger in your hand, then squeeze the juice over the crab. Leave the crab to marinate in the ginger juice. **two** Prepare the pasta. Put the flour in a bowl and make a well in the center. Beat the eggs with the vanilla extract and seeds, then pour into the flour. Bind to a stiff dough, then knead thoroughly. Roll out very thinly, or pass the dough through a pasta machine until thin enough to cut into spaghetti. Drape over a pole or the back of a chair on a cloth to dry until ready to cook. **three** Bring a large pan of salted water to a boil. Meanwhile, heat the oil in a skillet. Add the eggplant and chopped ginger and cook gently until soft and lightly browned. Add the pasta to the boiling water and cook just until it floats to the top of the water again, 1 to 2 minutes. Drain the pasta well and shake it dry. **four** Add the marinated crab and juice to the eggplant and heat for about 1 minute. Add the pasta, and toss the mixture together. Add the chopped tomato and season just before serving.

halibut with blackened eggplant butter

A VARIATION ON A TRADITIONAL FISH DISH WITH BLACK BUTTER;
THE EGGPLANT GIVES JUST A LITTLE MORE FLAVOR TO THE DISH.

serves four

4 Tbsp butter

2 Tbsp olive oil

1 small eggplant, cut into ¼-inch dice

1 garlic clove, crushed

2 Tbsp capers

1½ lb halibut fillets

Salt and freshly ground black pepper

1 Tbsp chopped fresh parsley

2 Tbsp lemon juice

one Heat the butter and oil together in a large skillet, then add the eggplant and cook over a moderate heat for 4 to 5 minutes, until softened and starting to brown. Add the garlic and capers and cook for another minute. Remove the vegetables from the pan with a slotted spoon, and keep warm. **two** Add the halibut to the skillet and cook for 3 to 4 minutes on each side, adding a little more butter only if absolutely necessary. Return the eggplant to the skillet just before the halibut is ready, season well and add the parsley with the lemon juice. **three** Serve the halibut with the eggplant butter spooned over.

braised squid with eggplant and asian vegetables

MANY PEOPLE ARE DISCOURAGED FROM EATING
SQUID BY THE RUBBERY TEXTURE THAT IS ALMOST SYNONYMOUS WITH BATTERED,
DEEP-FRIED SQUID RINGS. WHEN BRAISED, SQUID HAS A MELTINGLY TENDER TEXTURE, AND
LENDS ITSELF ESPECIALLY WELL TO CHINESE COOKING.

three to four

serves

3 Tbsp vegetable oil

1 lb prepared squid, defrosted if frozen, cut into rings and tentacles chopped

1 eggplant, sliced

1 large green bell pepper, cored, seeded, and cut into large pieces

1 large red bell pepper, cored, seeded, and cut into large pieces

12 oz Bok choy, cut into thick slices

1 large onion, roughly chopped

2 Tbsp cornstarch

1 cup water

½ cup sherry

½ cup soy sauce

one Heat the oil in a wok, then add the squid and fry quickly for 1 to 2 minutes until it becomes opaque. Remove from the wok with a slotted spoon and keep warm. **two** Add the eggplant to the wok and cook until lightly browned, adding a little extra oil if necessary, then add the remaining vegetables. Blend the cornstarch with a little of the water, then add to the wok with the remaining water, sherry and soy sauce. Bring to a boil, stirring all the time, then return the squid to the wok and mix with the vegetables. **three** Cover and simmer gently for 15 minutes. Serve immediately, with plain boiled rice or noodles.

red mullet fillets
with eggplants and
arugula pesto

A LIGHT FISH DISH WITH VERY ROBUST FLAVORS; RED

MULLET HAS A MEATY TASTE WHICH BALANCES THE PESTO VERY WELL.

serves four

2 eggplants, each cut lengthwise into
½-inch slices

Salt

2–3 Tbsp olive oil

8 large red mullet fillets

Pesto:

1 cup mixed arugula and parsley leaves,
about half and half

⅓ cup freshly grated Parmesan cheese

⅓ cup pine nuts

2 garlic cloves, crushed

½ cup olive oil

Salt and freshly ground black pepper

one Prepare the pesto. Place all the ingredients in a blender or food processor and blend to a smooth sauce. Season to taste, then turn into a small bowl. **two** Lay the eggplant slices in a single layer on a cookie sheet. Sprinkle with salt and leave for 30 minutes. Preheat the oven to 400°F. Rinse the eggplant well under cold water and dry on paper towels. Heat the oil in a griddle pan, add the eggplants and cook until browned on both sides. Remove and keep warm in the oven. **three** Add more oil to the griddle if necessary. Add the mullet fillets, skin side down, and cook for 1 to 2 minutes. Transfer the fish to a buttered cookie sheet and cook in the oven for 5 to 6 minutes. **four** To serve, arrange 2 eggplant slices on individual warmed serving plates, then place a mullet fillet on each. Spoon a little of the pesto onto the plates, then serve immediately.

deep-fried fish with eggplant couscous

YOU COULD USE ANY WHITE FISH FILLETS FOR THIS UNUSUAL RECIPE.

¼ cup olive oil

1 eggplant, cut into ¼-inch dice

1 tsp ground turmeric

½ cucumber, cut into ¼-inch dice

6 scallions, finely chopped

⅓ cup pistachio nuts, roughly chopped

⅓ cup dried apricots, finely chopped

1½ cups well-flavored vegetable broth

1 cup couscous

1 tsp white wine vinegar (optional)

Vegetable oil, for deep-frying

1 large egg white

2 Tbsp heavy cream

1 cup fine whole wheat flour

1 tsp chili powder

2 tsp ground cumin

Salt and freshly ground black pepper

1 lb filleted white fish, cut into 1-inch pieces

one Heat the olive oil in a skillet. Add the eggplant and turmeric and fry for 3 to 4 minutes, until soft. Turn into a bowl and add the cucumber, scallions, nuts, and apricots. **two** Bring the broth to a boil in a small pan, then add the couscous. Cover, remove from the heat and leave for 20 minutes. **three** Heat the oil for deep-frying in a large pan to 375°F. Meanwhile, whisk the egg white in a bowl until just frothy, then stir in the cream. Mix the flour on a flat plate with the spices and a little salt and pepper. Toss the fish in the egg and cream, rubbing the mixture into the flesh, then coat the pieces in the seasoned flour. **four** Deep-fry the fish in batches for about 3 minutes, then remove with a slotted spoon and drain on paper towels. **five** Stir the couscous into the vegetables and season well. Add a teaspoon of wine vinegar if you wish. Make a mound of couscous on each plate, then scatter with the deep-fried fish to serve.

almond-coated fish cakes with thai eggplant salad

DON'T BE PUT OFF BY THE NUMBER OF INGREDIENTS IN THIS RECIPE; IT IS VERY STRAIGHTFORWARD AND UTTERLY DELICIOUS.

serves four as a main course, eight as a appetizer

2¾ cups fresh white bread crumbs

1–2 Tbsp milk

3 Tbsp peanut oil

4 scallions, finely sliced

1 lb white fish fillets, skinned and cut into ¼-inch dice

1 large egg, beaten

1–2 Tbsp chopped cilantro

1 Tbsp chopped fresh parsley

Salt and white pepper

2–3 Tbsp mayonnaise

½ cup ground almonds

Salad:

2 long, thin Thai eggplants

1–2 hot Thai chiles, seeded and finely sliced

4 scallions, finely sliced

2 Tbsp fish sauce

juice of 2 lemons

½ piece lemon grass, bruised and finely sliced

2 lime leaves, finely shredded

2 Tbsp superfine sugar

¾ cup snow peas, shredded lengthwise

¾ cup baby corn, shredded lengthwise

one First make the salad. Cook the eggplants on a barbecue, under a broiler or in a hot oven until blackened and wrinkled, turning once or twice. Cover with a damp cloth and leave for 10 to 15 minutes, then peel off the skin. Chop the eggplant into large chunks, then add to all the other salad ingredients in a large bowl and leave to marinate for at least 30 minutes. **two** Soak 2 cups of the bread crumbs in the milk for a few minutes, then squeeze them dry and discard the milk. Heat 1 tablespoon of oil in a large skillet. Add the scallions and cook until soft but not browned. Remove with a slotted spoon and mix with the bread crumbs in a large bowl. Add the fish, egg, cilantro, and parsley. Season to taste, then add just enough mayonnaise to bind the mixture. **three** Mix together the remaining bread crumbs and almonds for the coating on a flat plate. Shape the fish mixture into 8 large fish cakes, then coat with the almond breadcrumbs, pressing the coating onto the fish cakes. **four** Heat the remaining oil in the skillet, then add the fish cakes and fry gently for 4 to 5 minutes on each side. Serve the fish cakes on a bed of the salad, with some of the salad juices spooned around.

eggplant
and cod bake

A SIMPLE BAKE WITH THE FLAVORS OF THE MEDITERRANEAN. I LIKE TO SERVE THIS WITH A CRISP GREEN SALAD AND CRUSTY FRENCH BREAD TO MOP UP THE JUICES.

serves four

Butter

Olive oil, for frying

1 eggplant, sliced

1 large onion, finely sliced

1 garlic clove, crushed

2 Tbsp capers

⅓ cup black pitted olives, Provençal if possible

2 cups canned chopped tomatoes

1 Tbsp chopped mixed fresh herbs, such as parsley, oregano, marjoram

Salt and freshly ground black pepper

Four 6 oz pieces of thick cod fillet, skinned

one Preheat the oven to 400°F. Butter an 8-inch round ovenproof serving dish. **two** Heat 2 to 3 tablespoons of oil in a large skillet and fry the eggplant slices gently until tender but not brown. Drain on paper towels. Add a little more oil if necessary, then add the onion and cook until softened and just starting to brown. Stir in the garlic, capers, and olives, then add the tomatoes, herbs, and seasoning to taste. Simmer the sauce for about 5 minutes, until it is slightly thickened and the onions are cooked. **three** Pour the sauce into the prepared dish, then nestle the cod fillets into it. Cover the fish with the eggplant slices and dot with butter. Place the dish on a cookie sheet if it seems very full and likely to bubble over, then bake in the hot oven for 20 minutes, until the eggplant slices are browned. Serve immediately.

meat
p
dish

and
oultry
es

roast chicken
with eggplant
paste

A SMOKY EGGPLANT PASTE FORCED UNDER THE SKIN OF A

CHICKEN BEFORE ROASTING HELPS TO KEEP IT MOIST. A LITTLE GROUND

TURMERIC ADDS EXTRA COLOR AND SPICE.

serves four to six

1 eggplant

Salt and freshly ground black pepper

2 carrots, cut into chunks

1 onion, cut in wedges

2 large zucchini, cut into chunks

1 green bell pepper, cored, seeded and cut into large pieces

1 garlic clove, halved

Olive oil, for drizzling

1 chicken, about 3½ lb

Pinch of ground turmeric

one Cook the eggplant over a barbecue, under a very hot broiler or in a hot oven until the skin is wrinkled and blistered and the flesh is tender. Turn once or twice during cooking. Cover with a damp cloth and leave for 10 minutes, until cool enough to handle. Peel off the skin, then mash the flesh with salt and pepper to a smooth paste. **two** Meanwhile, preheat the oven to 400°F. Place the vegetables and garlic in a roasting pan. Season them lightly and drizzle with olive oil. Carefully loosen the skin on the chicken breast and spread the breast with the eggplant paste, pushing it underneath the skin. Pat the skin back into position. Season the chicken well and sprinkle with a pinch of turmeric. Place the chicken on top of the vegetables. **three** Roast in the preheated oven for 1 hour, or until the juices run clear when you insert a skewer into the thigh. Remove the chicken, wrap it in aluminum foil and leave to stand for 20 minutes before carving. Meanwhile, return the vegetables to the oven to continue roasting for 20 minutes. **four** Carve the chicken, or cut it into portions, and serve with the roasted vegetables.

deep-fried eggplant and chicken strips

A GOOD SUPPER DISH TO SERVE WITH TARTARE SAUCE OR MAYONNAISE.

serves four

1 egg white

1 Tbsp heavy cream

Vegetable oil, for deep-frying

1 large eggplant, cut into thin strips

2 large chicken breasts, cut into thin strips

3 Tbsp sesame seeds

Salt

Lemon wedges, for serving

Spiced flour:

½ cup whole wheat flour

2 tsp ground cinnamon

2 tsp paprika

1 tsp salt

one Mix the flour with the spices and salt in a shallow dish. Beat the egg white until just frothy, then mix it with the cream. **two** Heat the oil for frying to 375°F in a large pan. Dip the eggplant and chicken strips in the cream mixture, then turn them in the seasoned flour to coat well. **three** Deep-fry the eggplant and chicken in batches until golden, then drain on paper towels. Scatter with sesame seeds and salt and serve with lemon wedges, and tartare sauce or mayonnaise.

meatballs with
eggplant and tomato
sauce

MEATBALLS MAKE A WELCOME CHANGE TO THE MORE USUAL GROUND BEEF SAUCE FOR PASTA. SIMMER THE MEATBALLS GENTLY TO PREVENT THEM FROM BREAKING UP DURING COOKING.

serves **four**

Meatballs:

1 lb ground lamb

6 scallions, finely chopped

1¼ cups fresh whole wheat bread crumbs

1 Tbsp tomato paste

½ tsp ground turmeric

Salt and freshly ground black pepper

1 large egg, beaten

Grated Parmesan for serving, optional

Sauce:

3 Tbsp olive oil

1 eggplant, cut into ½-inch chunks

1 onion, finely diced

1 garlic clove, finely sliced

½ tsp ground turmeric

1 tsp ground cumin

4 cups canned chopped tomatoes

1 bay leaf

Salt and freshly ground black pepper

8–10 fresh basil leaves, torn

one Mix all the ingredients for the meatballs together. Shape the mixture with wet hands into walnut-sized balls. **two** To make the sauce, heat the oil in a large skillet, then add the eggplant and fry gently until lightly golden. Add the meatballs, together with the onion, garlic, turmeric, and cumin, and cook until the meatballs are browned all over. Add extra oil only if the meatballs are sticking. **three** Add the tomatoes and bay leaf with salt and pepper and bring the mixture to the boil. Simmer gently for 20 minutes, then season to taste. Add the basil to the sauce just before serving. **four** Serve with pasta, sprinkling a little Parmesan over the meatballs if wished.

lamb and eggplant kabobs

THE RICH JUICES OF THE LAMB HELP TO MOISTEN AND FLAVOR THE EGGPLANT IN THESE DELICIOUS KABOBS. SERVE WITH RICE IF YOU PREFER, BUT THEY MAKE IDEAL PARTY OR BARBECUE FOOD WHEN SERVED IN WARM PITA BREAD.

serves **four to six**

1 lb boned leg or shoulder of lamb, cut into 1-inch cubes

1 large eggplant, cut into 1-inch cubes

Salt

12 cherry tomatoes

Lettuce leaves, to garnish

Marinade:

Grated rind and juice of 1 lemon

Grated rind and juice of 1 lime

1 Tbsp chopped cilantro

1 hot red chile, seeded if preferred, very finely chopped

Salt and freshly ground black pepper

2 Tbsp olive oil

Dressing:

⅔ cup sour cream

⅔ cup plain yogurt

3 Tbsp snipped chives

1 Tbsp chopped fresh parsley

one Place the lamb in a shallow dish. Mix all the ingredients for the marinade together, then pour the mixture over the lamb. Leave to marinate for at least 1 hour, stirring once or twice. **two** Place the eggplant in a colander and sprinkle with salt. Leave for at least 30 minutes, then rinse thoroughly with cold water. Pat dry on paper towels. **three** Mix all the ingredients for the dressing together, then spoon into a small serving bowl. **four** Drain the lamb, reserving the marinade, and thread onto 12 kabob skewers with the eggplant and tomatoes. Do not pack the pieces too closely together. Cook the kabobs on a barbecue or under a preheated broiler for 12 to15 minutes, turning occasionally and basting with the reserved marinade, until the lamb and eggplant are browned and tender. **five** Serve on the skewers or in warmed pita breads, with lettuce leaves and a spoonful of the dressing.

eggplant
stuffed with lamb
and couscous A FILLED BAKED EGGPLANT RECIPE THAT ONLY NEEDS

A SALAD TO ACCOMPANY IT. COUSCOUS MAKES AN EXCELLENT STUFFING FOR VEGETABLES.

serves four

1¼ cups well-flavored broth

Good pinch of saffron

1 cup couscous

2 eggplants

Salt and freshly ground black pepper

6 green cardamoms, lightly crushed and seeds removed

1 tsp ground ginger

2 garlic cloves

3 Tbsp olive oil, plus extra if necessary

1 large onion, finely chopped

½ lb lamb, finely sliced

1 green chile, seeded and chopped

½ cup ready-to-eat dried apricots, finely chopped

Butter, for greasing

one Bring the broth to a boil with the saffron. Pour in the couscous. Cover, remove from the heat and leave to stand. **two** Cut the eggplants in half lengthwise; do not remove the stalks as they will keep the eggplants in shape during cooking. Scoop out the flesh, leaving a shell about ¼ inch thick. Salt the shells lightly, then leave them upside down on paper towels to drain. Chop the flesh. **three** Grind the cardamom, ginger and garlic to a rough paste. Preheat the oven to 425°F. **four** Heat the oil in a pan, add the onion and spice paste and cook over a low heat until soft. Add the lamb, chile, and eggplant flesh and cook quickly until the lamb has browned. Stir in the couscous and chopped apricots. Season to taste. **five** Rinse the eggplant shells in cold water, then place in a buttered ovenproof dish. Pile the filling into the shells, then cover with buttered foil and bake for 20 minutes. Remove the foil and cook for a further 10 to 15 minutes, until the top is browned.

eggplant and turkey burgers

MY HUSBAND THOUGHT THERE OUGHT TO BE A BURGER RECIPE IN THIS BOOK, SO HERE IT IS! I HAVE TRIED TO CONJURE UP THE FLAVORS OF ITALY, USING DOLCELATTE IN THE BURGERS AND CIABATTA ROLLS TO HOLD THEM. DON'T FRY THE EGGPLANT SLICES IN TOO MUCH OIL, SO THAT THEY ARE VERY JUICY, OR THE BURGERS WILL BECOME SOFT AND VERY DIFFICULT TO EAT.

serves **four**

4 ciabatta rolls

14 oz lean, boned turkey or chicken, cut into strips

4 scallions, roughly chopped

½ cup crumbled dolcelatte or other blue-veined cheese

4 halves sun-dried tomatoes, roughly chopped

2 garlic cloves

Salt and freshly ground black pepper

Olive oil, for frying

4 large, thick eggplant slices

Lettuce leaves

Mustard or mayonnaise, for serving

one Warm the rolls in a low oven. **two** Process the turkey, scallions, cheese, tomatoes and garlic to a paste in a food processor, in two batches if necessary. Season the mixture, then shape into four flat burgers. **three** Heat 1 to 2 tablespoons of olive oil in a large skillet and add the burgers and eggplant slices. Fry gently for 4 to 5 minutes on each side, adding extra oil only if the burgers are sticking. **four** Split the warm rolls and place a slice of eggplant in the bottom of each. Top with a burger, some lettuce, and a dollop of mayonnaise or mustard. Cover with the top of the roll, then enjoy!

with potted ham eggplants

A RICH MOUSSE, SET IN INDIVIDUAL MOLDS LINED WITH EGGPLANT SLICES. SERVE WITH LOTS OF SALAD AND FRESH ROAST, OR BOILED NEW POTATOES.

serves **four**

2 large eggplants
Salt and freshly ground black pepper
⅔ cup milk
1 Tbsp butter
1 Tbsp all-purpose flour
2 tsp Dijon or pepper mustard
Olive oil, for frying and greasing
4 Tbsp dry white wine
1 tsp powdered gelatin
1 cup cooked chopped ham
⅔ cup heavy cream
1 Tbsp chopped fresh parsley

one Slice one eggplant very thinly. Lay the slices on a cookie sheet in a single layer, sprinkle with salt, then leave for 30 minutes. Cook the other eggplant over a barbecue, under a broiler or in a hot oven until the skin is wrinkled and blistered and the flesh is tender; turn once or twice during cooking. Cover with a damp cloth and leave for 10 to 15 minutes, then peel off the skin. **two** Heat the milk, butter, and flour together in a pan until thickened and boiling, stirring all the time. Add the mustard, salt and pepper, then cover with waxed paper to prevent a skin forming on the sauce and leave until cold. **three** Rinse the salted eggplant thoroughly and pat dry on paper towels. Heat a skillet or griddle pan, add a little oil, then cook the slices on both sides, a few at a time, until tender, adding more oil as necessary. Drain on paper towels and leave to cool. **four** Heat the wine in a small pan until bubbling, then remove from the heat and sprinkle on the gelatin. Stir to dissolve, then leave for 2 to 3 minutes. Oil 4 individual pudding bowls and line them with the eggplant slices, overlapping them slightly around the sides of the molds. **five** Cut the peeled eggplant into chunks, then purée it with the ham in a blender or food processor. Whip the cream until thick and floppy. Mix the cream and the ham mixture into the sauce, blending them all together well. Season with pepper as necessary; the ham should provide all the salt required. Stir the gelatin again, then fold it into the ham cream with the parsley. **six** Carefully spoon the ham into the prepared molds, banging them on the worktop to shake the mixture down. Chill for at least 2 hours before turning out the molds onto individual plates.

venison sausage and eggplant casserole

I LIKE TO USE VENISON SAUSAGES FOR THIS CASSEROLE, BUT YOU CAN USE HERBY OR SPICY SAUSAGES, WHICHEVER YOU PREFER.

serves **four**

2 Tbsp olive oil

8 thick venison sausages

2 slices smoked bacon, diced

1 large onion, finely chopped

1 carrot, diced

1–2 garlic cloves, sliced

⅔ cup red wine

1 large eggplant, cut into ½-inch chunks

2 cups canned chopped tomatoes

½ cup French lentils

1 Tbsp tomato paste

1¼ cups beef broth

Salt and freshly ground black pepper

Parsley sprigs, to garnish

one Preheat the oven to 350°F. Heat the oil in a flameproof casserole, then add the sausages and cook them briefly until browned all over. Add the bacon, onion, carrot, and garlic, then cover the casserole and cook slowly for 4 to 5 minutes. **two** Add the red wine, then cook rapidly until it is well reduced. Add all the remaining ingredients, then bring to a boil. Cover and cook in the preheated oven for 1 hour. **three** Season to taste, then garnish with parsley just before serving.

pork and mushroom stuffed eggplants

USE SMALL PURPLE OR STRIPED EGGPLANTS FOR THIS DISH, IF AVAILABLE. I LIKE TO MAKE A FRESH TOMATO SAUCE TO SERVE WITH IT, MAKING FULL USE OF THE HOT OVEN WHILE IT IS ON TO BAKE THE EGGPLANTS.

serves **four**

4 small eggplants, round ones if possible, or 2 larger ones

Salt

4 Tbsp olive oil

1 large onion, finely chopped

4 rashers unsmoked bacon, chopped

1 garlic clove, crushed

½ lb ground pork

1 tsp paprika

4 oz mushrooms

1 Tbsp tomato paste

Salt and freshly ground black pepper

8–12 basil leaves, roughly torn

Stock, wine or water

Sauce:

8 ripe tomatoes, halved

1 small onion, quartered

2 garlic cloves, peeled but left whole

1 Tbsp light brown sugar

Olive oil, to drizzle

one Preheat the oven to 450°F. Cut off the tops of the eggplants, if using round ones, and scoop out the flesh, leaving a shell about ¼ inch thick. If using larger eggplants, halve them, and scoop out the flesh. Salt lightly, then leave the shells upside down on paper towels to drain. Chop the flesh finely. **two** Heat the oil in a pan. Add the onion and cook over a low heat with the bacon and garlic for about 5 minutes, then add the ground pork and paprika. Cook quickly until browned, then add half the eggplant flesh and mushrooms and cook for a further 2 to 3 minutes. **three** Season the mixture, adding the tomato paste and basil with salt and black pepper. Add a little stock, wine or water, if necessary, to moisten the mixture, then leave to simmer gently. Rinse the eggplant shells thoroughly in cold water and drain. Pack the filling into them, then place in a buttered ovenproof dish. Cover with foil. **four** Arrange the sauce ingredients in a single layer in a roasting pan with the remaining eggplant flesh. Season well, adding the sugar and a drizzle of olive oil. Cook the sauce at the top of the oven with the eggplants underneath for 35 to 40 minutes, until the tomatoes have started to blacken. **five** Remove the sauce ingredients from the oven and allow to cool slightly. Remove the foil from the eggplants and return to the oven until the sauce is completed. Tip all the roasted vegetables and their juices into a blender and process until smooth. Press the purée through a sieve with the back of a spoon to give a smooth sauce, then season to taste. Serve the stuffed eggplants with the tomato sauce.

rich eggplant ragout for pasta

THERE ARE SPAGHETTI SAUCES, AND THEN THERE ARE RICH, FLAVORSOME RAGOUTS. I USE A MIXTURE OF MEATS FOR THIS SAUCE, AND ADD EGGPLANT FOR EXTRA RICHNESS. SERVE WITH SPAGHETTI, TAGLIATELLE OR ANY FLAT PASTA.

serves **six to eight**

4 Tbsp olive oil
1 large onion, finely chopped
1 eggplant, cut into ½-inch chunks
1¼ cups ground beef
1¼ cups ground pork
½ lb chicken livers, finely chopped
⅔ cup red wine
4 cups canned chopped tomatoes
1 Tbsp tomato paste
2 garlic cloves, finely sliced
2–3 bay leaves
Salt and freshly ground black pepper
Freshly grated nutmeg, to taste

one Heat half the olive oil in a large pan. Add the onion and cook for 4 to 5 minutes over a low heat until soft and transparent. Add the remaining oil and the eggplant, then cook quickly until the eggplant starts to brown. Stir in the meat and chicken livers and continue cooking over a medium-high heat until all the meat is browned. **two** Pour the wine into the pan and cook over a high heat until it has almost evaporated, stirring all the time to scrape up any sediment from the bottom of the pan. Lower the heat, then add all the remaining ingredients. Bring to the boil, then cook for at least 1 hour at a very slow simmer. If preferred, cover the pan and cook for 1 to 2 hours in a slow oven at 325°F. **three** Season the râgout to taste. Serve as a pasta sauce with spaghetti or tagliatelle, use as a sauce for lasagne, or top with creamy potatoes mashed with olive oil and garlic for a cottage pie with a difference!

veget

able
dishes

imam bayaldi –
the Imam fainted

THIS IS A CLASSIC DISH, ALTHOUGH I HAVE FOUND MANY DIFFERING RECIPES FOR IT, SO HERE'S MINE! THE TITLE COMES FROM THE LEGEND THAT THE IMAM, OR HOLY MAN, WAS OVERCOME BY THE DELICIOUS AROMA WHEN THIS WAS FIRST COOKED FOR HIM!

serves four

4 large eggplants
Salt
⅔ cup fruity olive oil
Juice of 1 lemon
1 tsp superfine sugar
About 2½ cups thick tomato juice

Stuffing:

½ lb tomatoes, skinned, seeded and chopped
1 large onion, finely chopped
3 Tbsp chopped fresh parsley
Salt and freshly ground black pepper
1 tsp ground cinnamon

one Score the flesh on the eggplants every ½ inch. Pare away alternate strips of skin, to make stripes. Stand the eggplants in a colander, sprinkle with salt and leave for 30 to 60 minutes. Rinse well under cold running water, then dry on paper towels. **two** Combine all the ingredients for the stuffing. Slit the eggplants on one side and pack the stuffing into them, then place in a covered skillet or sauté pan, slit side uppermost. **three** Pour the oil and lemon juice over the eggplants and sprinkle with the sugar. Add enough tomato juice to just cover them. Cover the pan and simmer slowly for about 1 hour, until the eggplants are soft. Alternatively, bake them for about 1 hour at 325°F. **four** Season the sauce once the eggplants are cooked, then allow them to cool completely. Chill for about 1 hour, then serve with the tomato sauce spooned over, accompanied by a rice salad or salad leaves.

eggplant and kidney bean chili

EGGPLANTS MAKE A GOOD ALTERNATIVE TO LENTILS FOR A VEGETABLE-BASED CHILI SAUCE. THE SPICING IN THIS IS QUITE STRONG; USE A LITTLE LESS CHILI POWDER IF YOU PREFER. SERVE WITH BROWN RICE OR TORTILLA CHIPS, AND AN AVOCADO DIP.

serves **four**

3 Tbsp peanut oil

1 large onion, chopped

2 tsp chili powder

1 tsp ground cumin

1 large eggplant, cut into ½-inch chunks

1–2 garlic cloves, crushed

1 large cinnamon stick

2 bay leaves

3 cups puréed tomatoes or thick tomato juice

Salt and freshly ground black pepper

2 cups canned red kidney beans and juice

Boiled rice, to serve

Sour cream and fresh cilantro leaves, to garnish

one Heat the oil in a large pan. Add the onion with the chili powder and cumin and cook for 4 to 5 minutes over a low heat, until the onion is soft but not browned. It is important to cook the onion slowly so that the spices do not burn. **two** Add the eggplant and garlic, and cook for 1 to 2 minutes, then add the cinnamon and bay leaves with the puréed tomatoes or tomato juice. Add salt and pepper, then bring to the boil. Cover the pan and simmer the sauce slowly for 10 minutes, then add the kidney beans and their juice. Continue cooking for a further 10 minutes, then remove the cinnamon and bay leaves. **three** Season the chile to taste, then serve on a bed of rice with a large spoonful of sour cream, garnished with cilantro.

eggplant and sweet potato curry

THIS MAKES A VERY SUBSTANTIAL MAIN COURSE, BUT IT COULD ALSO BE SERVED AS A SIDE DISH WITH MEAT OR FISH CURRIES.

serves four

2 tsp cumin seeds

1 Tbsp mustard seeds

3 Tbsp ghee or sunflower oil

2 small sweet potatoes, about 1 lb, peeled and cut into ½-inch chunks

1 large onion, finely sliced

2 garlic cloves, finely sliced

1–2 tsp chili powder

1 tsp ground turmeric

1 large eggplant, cut the same size as the potato

1 Tbsp blue poppy seeds

1 cup water or vegetable broth

2 tsp salt

1 Tbsp torn fresh cilantro leaves

one Heat a large skillet over a medium heat, then add the cumin and mustard seeds and dry-fry for 30 seconds or so, until aromatic and starting to pop. Transfer to a plate and leave to cool. **two** Heat the ghee or oil in the pan, add the potatoes and cook for 3 to 4 minutes until starting to soften. Add the onion, garlic, chili powder, and turmeric and cook for 1 to 2 minutes, then add the eggplant with the roasted spices and the poppy seeds. Stir in the water and salt, then cover and simmer very slowly for 30 to 45 minutes, until the vegetables are tender. **three** Season the curry to taste, then serve sprinkled with the cilantro.

eggplant and almond rissoles

RISSOLE IS A VERY OLD-FASHIONED WORD, BUT I LOVE THESE LITTLE PATTIES WITH A SIDE SALAD AND TARTARE SAUCE, OR EVEN TOMATO KETCHUP IF I'M BY MYSELF.

serves **four**

1 large eggplant
⅔ cup milk
1 Tbsp butter
1 heaped Tbsp whole wheat flour
Salt and freshly ground black pepper
4 scallions, finely chopped
1 Tbsp chopped fresh oregano
½ cup ground almonds
1⅓ cups fresh whole wheat bread crumbs
½ cup olive oil
2 eggs, beaten
1 cup dry whole wheat bread crumbs, toasted – you will need more if you make your own toasted crumbs
Tartare sauce and salad, to serve

one Cook the eggplant on a barbecue, under a broiler or in a hot oven until the skin is wrinkled and blistered and the flesh is tender, turning once or twice. Cover with a damp cloth and leave for 10 to 15 minutes, then peel off the skin and chop the flesh roughly. **two** Heat the milk, butter and flour together, stirring all the time, until thickened and boiling. Cook for 1 to 2 minutes, then season to taste and turn into a large bowl. Blend the eggplant with the scallions and oregano, then add it to the sauce. Add the almonds, more seasoning and bread crumbs to give a thick, manageable paste. Shape into 8 rissoles, flouring your hands as necessary. **three** Heat the oil in a large skillet. Dip each rissole in the beaten egg and then the toasted bread crumbs, pressing on the crumbs. Add the rissoles to the pan and fry gently for 4 to 5 minutes on each side. Serve immediately, with tartare sauce and salad.

eggplant and
tomato galette

I LIKE TO SERVE THIS AS A SUPPER DISH BUT IT COULD EASILY
STRETCH TO FEED MORE AS AN APPETIZER. ALTHOUGH IT TAKES SOME TIME TO PREPARE,
THE WORK CAN BE DONE IN ADVANCE, AND THEN BAKED AT THE LAST MOMENT.

serves **four**

Butter, for greasing
6 large eggs, beaten
¼ cup milk
Salt and freshly ground black pepper
1 large eggplant, sliced
Olive oil, for frying
4 tomatoes, sliced
1-2 garlic cloves, thinly sliced
¼ lb mozzarella, thinly sliced
Sauce:
⅔ cup sour cream
⅔ cup plain yogurt
2 Tbsp chopped chives
Grated rind and juice of ½ lemon

one Preheat the oven to 400°F, and grease a round gratin dish, the same diameter as your omelet pan. Beat the eggs with the milk and a little seasoning, then use to make three fairly thick omelets. Stack the finished omelets on paper towels until required. (I finish the top of each omelet under a hot broiler, to save turning them over in the pan.). **two** Heat 2 to 3 tablespoons of olive oil in a skillet. Add the eggplant and cook until just tender and lightly browned, adding more oil as necessary. Place one omelet in the bottom of the dish, then arrange half the eggplant slices in a layer on top. Season, then cover with half the sliced tomatoes and garlic. Season again and top with a third of the mozzarella. Repeat the layers, finishing with an omelet topped with mozzarella. **three** Bake in the preheated oven for 20 to 25 minutes, until the galette is piping hot and the mozzarella has melted and lightly browned. **four** Mix all the ingredients for the sauce together while the galette is baking. Serve the galette cut into quarters, with the sauce spooned over.

eggplant and peppers, szechuan-style

SZECHUAN COOKING IS VERY SPICED. YOU COULD SERVE THIS AS A MAIN COURSE BY ITSELF, OR WITH A MEAT OR FISH DISH.

serves **three to four**

Peanut oil, for frying

1 large eggplant, cut into 1-inch chunks

2 garlic cloves, crushed

2-inch piece fresh gingerroot, peeled and very finely chopped

1 onion, roughly chopped

2 green bell peppers, cored, seeded and cut into 1-inch pieces

1 red bell pepper, cored, seeded and cut into 1-inch pieces

1 hot red chile, seeded and finely shredded

½ cup well-flavored vegetable broth

1 Tbsp granulated sugar

1 tsp rice or white wine vinegar

Salt and freshly ground black pepper

1 tsp cornstarch

1 Tbsp light soy sauce

Sesame oil, for sprinkling

one Heat 3 tablespoons of oil in a wok. Add the eggplant and stir-fry for 4 to 5 minutes, until lightly browned. Add more oil if necessary. Remove the eggplant with a slotted spoon and keep warm. **two** Add a little more oil to the wok, then add the garlic and ginger and fry for just a few seconds before adding the onions and peppers with the chile. Stir-fry for 2 to 3 minutes, then return the eggplant to the wok with the remaining ingredients. **three** Continue to stir-fry until the sauce has boiled and thickened, at which stage the cornstarch will clear. Check the seasoning, adding a little more salt or soy sauce as necessary, then serve immediately sprinkled with sesame oil, with boiled or fried rice.

lentil
moussaka
A MEATLESS VARIATION OF THE CLASSIC BAKED DISH. THIS IS RICH,

FILLING, AND FULL OF FIBER, SO IT MUST BE GOOD FOR YOU!

serves four to six

Olive oil, for frying

1 large onion, chopped

2 garlic cloves, crushed

1 green bell pepper, cored and chopped

1 cup red lentils

About ⅔ cup red wine

2 cups canned chopped tomatoes

Salt and freshly ground black pepper

1 Tbsp chopped fresh oregano

2 large eggplants, sliced

2½ cups milk

4 Tbsp butter, plus extra for greasing

4 Tbsp all-purpose flour

1 cup grated Cheddar cheese

one Preheat the oven to 425°F. Heat 2 tablespoons of oil in a large pan. Add the onion, garlic, and pepper and cook gently until soft. Add the lentils, red wine, and tomatoes. Bring to a boil, then season and add the oregano. Simmer for 20 minutes, or until the lentils are soft. Add a little more wine to the sauce if it seems dry. **two** Meanwhile, heat 2 to 3 tablespoons of oil in a large skillet. Fry the eggplant slices on both sides until tender, adding more oil if necessary, then drain on paper towels. Add any oil left in the skillet to the lentil sauce. **three** Heat the milk, butter and flour together in a pan, stirring all the time, until boiling and thickened. Continue to cook for 1 minute, to remove the taste of flour from the sauce, then remove the pan from the heat. Add all but 2 tablespoons of the grated cheese and then season to taste. **four** Layer the lentil sauce and eggplant slices in a buttered, ovenproof dish, finishing with a layer of eggplant. Spoon the sauce over the eggplants, then scatter the remaining cheese over the top. Bake in the preheated oven for 30 minutes, until the moussaka is browned and set. Serve immediately with a salad and garlic bread.

eggplant and tomato gratin

POTATOES TURN THIS GRATIN INTO A SUBSTANTIAL SUPPER DISH.

serves **four**

Olive oil, for frying
2 large eggplants, thickly sliced
1 large onion, chopped
1 lb potatoes, peeled and thickly sliced
2 garlic cloves, finely sliced
Salt and freshly ground black pepper
8 ripe tomatoes, sliced
⅔ cup well-flavored broth
1 cup mixed grated cheeses,
½ cup fresh bread crumbs

one Heat 2 to 3 tablespoons of the oil in a large pan, add the eggplant slices and fry until lightly browned on both sides. Remove them with a slotted spoon. Add the onion and sliced potatoes to the pan, with a little extra oil if necessary, and cook until starting to soften. Stir in the garlic and season to taste. Return the eggplants to the pan with the sliced tomatoes, add the broth, then cover the pan and cook slowly for 30 minutes, or until all the vegetables are tender. Season to taste. **two** Turn the vegetables into a buttered, ovenproof gratin dish, with as much of the cooking liquor as you wish. Preheat the broiler. Mix the cheeses with the bread crumbs and scatter them over the vegetables. Broil until the cheese has melted and browned. Serve immediately.

eggplant and zucchini spaghetti

A VERY SIMPLE BUT SPECIAL RECIPE.

serves **four**

Salt and freshly ground black pepper
Olive oil, for frying
⅓ cup pine nuts
1 large eggplant, sliced
12 oz dried spaghetti
2 large zucchini, sliced
1–2 garlic cloves, crushed
2 Tbsp torn basil leaves and chopped fresh parsley, mixed
Freshly grated Parmesan cheese, to serve

one Bring a large pan of salted water to a boil. Heat a little oil in a large skillet, add the pine nuts and cook until golden. Remove with a slotted spoon and leave on a plate, then add the eggplant with more oil and fry until starting to soften and brown. Meanwhile, add the pasta to the boiling water, return to a boil and simmer for 10 to 12 minutes, or until *al dente*. **two** Add the zucchini and garlic to the skillet and continue frying until all the vegetables are soft and golden; this will take about 8 to 10 minutes. **three** Drain the pasta and add it to the skillet with the herbs. Season to taste. You shouldn't need to add any extra oil at this stage as some will run from the cooked vegetables. Add the pine nuts and toss well. Serve immediately, with grated Parmesan.

mixed vegetable
gumbo
GUMBO IS A TRADITIONAL DISH OF OKRA AND SPICES FROM THE
SOUTHERN STATES OF THE USA. IT USUALLY CONTAINS CHICKEN OR FISH, BUT I OFTEN
MAKE IT WITH JUST A GOOD SELECTION OF VEGETABLES FOR VEGETARIAN FRIENDS.

serves four

⅔ cup olive oil, plus extra if needed

2 large onions, chopped

1 red bell pepper, cored, seeded, and cut into ½-inch squares

1 green bell pepper, cored, seeded and cut into ½-inch squares

1 hot chile, green or red, seeded and finely sliced

2 garlic cloves, finely sliced

1 lb okra, cut into ½-inch slices

2 cups canned chopped tomatoes

2 Tbsp butter

3 Tbsp all-purpose flour

2 tsp chili powder

1 tsp ground cumin

3½ cups well-flavored vegetable broth

4–5 sprigs fresh thyme

Salt and freshly ground black pepper

1 large eggplant, cut into 1-inch pieces

1 long, thin eggplant, finely sliced

½ cup long-grain rice

one Heat 3 tablespoons of the oil in a large pan. Add the onion and cook gently until softened but not browned, then add the peppers, chile, garlic, and okra. Cook for about 5 minutes over a very low heat, then add the tomatoes. Cover the pan and simmer slowly for 15 minutes. **two** Meanwhile, melt the butter in a large flameproof casserole, then add the flour and spices and cook over a low heat until bubbling gently. Remove from the heat and gradually add the broth, stirring all the time, then add the thyme. Return to the heat and bring slowly to a boil. Simmer the sauce for 1 to 2 minutes; it should be quite thin, even after boiling. Season well, then add the vegetable mixture. Cover the pan and cook slowly for 30 minutes. **three** Meanwhile, heat the remaining oil in a large skillet, add the chopped eggplant and fry until browned, stirring the pieces gently so that they do not break up in the pan. Transfer to the gumbo with a slotted spoon and simmer for a further 15 minutes. **four** Boil the rice in salted water until tender, then drain. Meanwhile, add the eggplant slices to the skillet, and cook until tender, adding a little extra oil if required. **five** Season the gumbo to taste. Serve with the rice and fried eggplant.

eggplant
and chili-stuffed
tortillas

FLOUR TORTILLAS TURN ALMOST ANY COMBINATION OF INGREDIENTS INTO A QUICK TEX-MEX MEAL. YOU COULD USE CHOPPED SCALLIONS OR AVOCADO AS ADDITIONAL SALAD GARNISHES. LEAVE THE CHILE UNSEEDED IF YOU LIKE YOUR TORTILLAS HOT.

serves **four**

1 large eggplant, cut into ½-inch chunks
1 onion, finely chopped
1 tsp chili powder
⅓ cup peanut oil
1 green chile, seeded and chopped
1 garlic clove, finely chopped
½ cup pecan nuts, roughly chopped
8 flour tortillas, warmed in a microwave
or in the oven according to directions

To serve:
Grated Cheddar cheese
Shredded lettuce
Chopped tomatoes
Sour cream

one Toss the eggplant and onion in the chili powder. Heat the oil in a large skillet, add the eggplant and onion and fry gently until lightly browned on all sides, about 5 minutes. Add the chile, garlic, and pecans and continue cooking for a further 5 minutes, or until all the vegetables are tender. **two** Meanwhile, heat the flour tortillas, either in the oven or in a microwave according to the instructions on the packet. **three** To serve, place some of the eggplant mixture in the center of each tortilla, then top with a little cheese, lettuce, sour cream, and tomatoes. Fold the bottom of the tortilla upward, then roll the sides over to enclose the filling.

eggplant cracked wheat pilaf

I LOVE TO COOK WITH CRACKED WHEAT AS IT RETAINS A GRAINY TEXTURE AND A NUTTY FLAVOR. THE COMBINATION OF EGGPLANT, FENNEL AND BELL PEPPERS WORKS VERY WELL INDEED.

serves four

Olive oil, for frying

1 large onion, chopped

1 fennel bulb, trimmed and sliced

1 eggplant, cut into large dice

1 green bell pepper, cored and chopped

1½ cups cracked wheat or bulgar wheat

2 cups canned chopped tomatoes

3 cups well-flavored broth

Salt and freshly ground black pepper

one Heat 2–3 tablespoons of the oil in a large skillet, add the onion and fennel and cook until just starting to soften. Stir in the eggplant and pepper, then cook for a minute or so before adding the wheat. Add the tomatoes and broth, then bring the pilaf to a boil. **two** Simmer for 15–20 minutes, until the broth has been absorbed. Season well with salt and pepper, then serve with a crisp green salad.

eggplant with garlic and tomatoes

A QUICK AND SIMPLE DISH TO COOK WHEN TIME IS SHORT.

serves two

1 eggplant, sliced

1 large onion, sliced

1–2 tsp paprika

⅓ cup olive oil

4 garlic cloves, peeled but left whole

8 halves of sun-dried tomatoes in oil, shredded finely

2 Tbsp oil from the tomatoes

Salt and freshly ground black pepper

2–3 Tbsp chopped fresh parsley

one Toss the eggplant and onion in the paprika. Heat the oil in a large skillet, add the eggplant and onion and cook for 3–4 minutes. Add the garlic and cook for 2–3 minutes, then add the tomatoes and their oil. **two** Continue to stir-fry for 8–10 minutes, until the eggplant is tender, and the onion and garlic have caramelized slightly. Season well, then add the parsley. Serve with plenty of bread and a green leaf salad.

re

lishes

eggplant and mango chutney

THIS IS A SWEET BUT HOT CHUTNEY, IDEAL FOR SERVING WITH CURRIES, OR WITH BREAD AND CHEESE.

makes about 4 x 1 lb jars

4 small green mangoes, ripe but firm, peeled and cut into chunks

2 eggplants, cut into 1-inch chunks

2–3 garlic cloves, crushed

2 hot red chiles, finely chopped

¾ cup finely chopped fresh gingerroot

1 Tbsp chili powder

1 Tbsp coarse sea salt

2½ cups distilled malt vinegar

5½ cups light brown sugar

one Layer the mangoes and eggplants in a colander, salting them lightly. Leave for 1 hour, then rinse well in cold water and drain. **two** Place the mangoes and eggplants in a large pan with all the remaining ingredients. Bring slowly to a boil, then cook gently for 45 to 60 minutes, until the chutney is well reduced but still juicily moist. **three** Pour into warmed jars, packing the mixture well down, then seal and label. Leave for 3 to 4 weeks to mature before eating.

eggplant salsa

MOST SALSAS ARE MADE WITH RAW VEGETABLES, SO THIS IS AN UNUSUAL COMBINATION OF HALF COOKED AND HALF RAW VEGETABLES.

serves four

4 Tbsp olive oil

1 large eggplant, cut into ¼-inch dice

1 red onion, finely chopped

4 red tomatoes, seeded and chopped

2 yellow tomatoes, seeded and chopped

1 chile, seeded and chopped

1 avocado, peeled and cut into chunks

Grated rind and juice of 1 lime

Salt and freshly ground black pepper

3 Tbsp freshly chopped cilantro

one Heat the oil in a pan. Add the eggplant and cook until browned and tender, then remove with a slotted spoon and place in a bowl. Allow the eggplant to cool. Reserve any oil left in the pan. **two** Add all the remaining ingredients to the bowl, tossing the avocado in the lime juice. Season well, then stir in any remaining oil and the cilantro. Allow to stand for at least 30 minutes before serving, to develop the flavors.

eggplants
preserved with
mint

THIS RECIPE IS BASED ON AN ARGENTINIAN RELISH, ALTHOUGH I SUSPECT THAT SIMILAR PRESERVES ARE EATEN THROUGHOUT THE MIDDLE EAST. TRY TO USE PRESERVING JARS FOR THIS RECIPE, WHICH THEN MAKE EXCELLENT PRESENTS. THE EGGPLANTS MUST REMAIN COMPLETELY COVERED BY THE OIL TO BE PROPERLY PRESERVED.

makes about **4 ¹/₄ lbs**

2 lb 4 oz small, fresh eggplants

Salt

2½ cups white wine vinegar

6-8 garlic cloves, according to size, finely sliced

¾ cup fresh mint leaves, left whole

1 Tbsp mixed peppercorns

2 large green chiles, seeded and finely shredded

2 cups fruity extra virgin olive oil

one Cut the eggplants into quarters lengthwise, then cut them into 2-inch chunks. Layer them in a colander with plenty of salt, then leave to stand for 2 to 3 hours, or even overnight. Rinse thoroughly under cold running water, then drain and shake dry. **two** Bring the vinegar to a boil in a deep pan, then add the eggplants and garlic and boil for 5 minutes. Stir once or twice, to keep the eggplants covered with the vinegar. Drain and allow to cool completely. **three** Layer the eggplants and garlic alternately with the mint in 1 large or 2 smaller warm, clean preserving jars. Season each layer with a mixture of the peppercorns and sliced chilis, and pack the layers tightly by pressing down firmly with a wooden spoon. **four** Pour half the oil into the jars, which will just about cover the eggplants, then cover and leave overnight. By the next day, the eggplants will have absorbed much of the oil. Add sufficient extra oil to cover the eggplants completely, then seal the jars and leave for at least a week before serving. Keep refrigerated, and use within 2 weeks.

indian-style
eggplant relish
MOST INDIAN RELISHES CONTAIN A LARGE QUANTITY OF OIL
AND ARE VERY HOT, AND THIS IS NO EXCEPTION. IT IS AN EXCELLENT RELISH TO ADD IN
SMALL QUANTITIES TO SHRIMP CURRIES.

makes about **2 ¼ lbs**

1 lb firm young eggplants, cut into 1-inch chunks

Salt

1 Tbsp cumin seeds

1¼ cups peanut oil

2 large onions, chopped

4 garlic cloves, finely chopped

2-inch piece fresh gingerroot, peeled and finely chopped

1 tsp ground turmeric

2 Tbsp light brown sugar

4 hot red chiles, finely sliced

2 green chiles, finely sliced

one Layer the eggplant in a colander with salt and leave for at least 1 hour. Rinse thoroughly under cold running water, then pat dry on paper towels. **two** Heat a large skillet over moderate heat, then add the cumin seeds and dry fry them for 30 seconds, until fragrant and just starting to color. Tip onto a plate and leave to cool. **three** Heat the oil in the skillet. Add the eggplants and onion and cook for 3 to 4 minutes, then add the garlic, ginger, and turmeric and continue cooking for a further 2 minutes. Allow to cool slightly, then mix the sugar into the oil with 1 teaspoon of salt. **four** Pack the eggplants and onions into warmed jars, layering them with the sliced chiles. Press down firmly on each layer with the back of a spoon to exclude all air from the jars. Pour as much of the oil into the jars as possible, then seal. **five** Keep the relish 2 weeks before using; store in the refrigerator but use within a month for the best flavor.

stuffed parathas

THESE FLATBREADS ARE ALMOST A MEAL IN THEMSELVES. SERVE WITH ANY SPICED DISH, OR AS A TASTY SNACK IN THEIR OWN RIGHT.

makes **six**

3 cups whole wheat flour, plus extra for dusting

½ tsp salt

About 1¼ cups water

vegetable oil or melted ghee, for frying

1–2 Tbsp butter

Yogurt or relish, to serve

Filling:

3 Tbsp vegetable or peanut oil

1 eggplant, cut into ¼-inch dice

½ tsp chili powder

½ tsp ground turmeric

1 Tbsp finely chopped fresh gingerroot

2 green chiles, seeded and finely chopped

2 Tbsp chopped fresh cilantro

1 tsp salt

one First make the filling. Heat the oil in a pan. Add the eggplant with the chili powder and turmeric and cook until soft, then add the remaining ingredients for the filling and mix well. Remove from the heat and leave to cool. **two** Mix the flour and salt to a firm manageable dough with cold water, then knead until pliable. Cover with a bowl and leave for 10 minutes. **three** Divide the dough into 6 pieces. Work with one piece of dough at a time, leaving the others covered until required. Roll out to a circle about 4 inches in diameter, then place some filling on the dough. Fold the edges over to enclose the filling, then dip the dough in a little extra flour and roll it out into a circle about 7 inches in diameter. The eggplant may break through the dough; try not to press too hard on the edges of the dough when rolling. If necessary, sprinkle a little extra flour over the dough to hold the filling. **four** Heat a griddle or large skillet over a moderate heat, then cook the parathas briefly for about 1 minute on each side. Brush each side with melted ghee or oil and cook gently until lightly browned and crisp. Keep the parathas warm wrapped in a clean cloth in a very low oven until they are all cooked. Serve hot, dotted with butter and with a spoonful of yogurt or relish.